WordPress

Basic Fundamental Guide for Beginners

TABLE OF CONTENTS

Introduction

Congratulations on downloading *WordPress: Basic Fundamental Guide For Beginners* and thank you for doing so.

The following chapters will discuss everything from what WordPress is and how it got started to the basics of building a website and staring to blog. In each chapter, there is detailed information that will help you along the way to building a WordPress website. Chapter one talks all about what WordPress is and how to make it work for you. It discusses how to set up a WordPress site and where in the c-Panel you would find the WordPress download that must be installed to you hosting site.

In chapter two we talk about what you need to know to utilize WordPress for your benefit. This is a short chapter because we have so much information in the other chapters that this one could be concise.

In chapter 3 you will learn how to change your WordPress theme, but that isn't all. You will also learn how you can find the perfect theme for your website, and customization features that will help make your website as professional as it can be. There is detailed information on each section of the customization process and how you can use it to build and design a wonderful site.

Chapter 4 talks about the plugins that are necessary to make your website run at optimal speed, as well as ones that help you with SEO, newsletter sign ups, contact forms, post and web page design, and antispam features. Each one of the plugins written about in this chapter are ones that are necessary for your website to run properly.

Chapter 5 is all about designing a beautiful website and the features that can be used on WordPress. It also talks about what a static page is and how it can help your business.

Chapter 6 has details about writing a blog with WordPress. It details exactly what a blog is and why people choose to write blogs. How to write one with WordPress and some HTML code that will help you with your blogs posts is also covered in this section. Included in this chapter are also details on the difference between visual and text mode and how each one is designed to help you with your writing needs.

There is so much information included in this book that by the time you finish reading it you should have no qualms about starting your WordPress website and blog.

There are plenty of books on this subject on the market, so thanks again for choosing this one! Every effort was made to ensure it is full of as much useful information as possible. Please enjoy!

This book contains proven steps and strategies on how to become a fantastic Arduino programmer from the base that we already built in the beginner book. However, even if you didn't get that book, don't worry; we're going to spend a chapter getting you up to speed so that you feel confident jumping into the higher level knowledge further in the book.

Arduino is an extremely cool and powerful tool for people who were born tinkerers. You'll be able to create really awesome programs and projects that are powered by a tiny computer. The world of hardware is now your oyster. This book is going to teach you to harness the full potential of the Arduino so that you can be an absolute sketch-master.

Thanks again for purchasing this book, I hope you enjoy it!

Chapter 1

What WordPress Is And
How To Make It Work For You

WordPress is a content management system. What this means is that WordPress is a website and blogging platform which allows you the freedom to customize your website without having to learn HTML, CSS, or Flash. With WordPress, you can use a simple system of drag and drop that will allow you to customize your theme, your layout, and your content.

WordPress made its debut in May of 2003. Matt Mullenweg and Mike Little started WordPress with the intentions of continuing the availability of a blogging platform. In 2003 the first content management system was b2 Cafelog. The original WordPress was loosely based on the b2 Cafelog, however, it had significant advancements and improvements to the b2 Cafelog. The first WordPress had a new admin interface, some new templates, and generated some XHTML 1.1 compliant templates. They released the 1.2 WordPress in 2004 and from that point on they continued to advance the blogging platform year after year.

When WordPress came out many people were amazed at the ability to create their own blog with so many new features and templates. WordPress became a place where they could express themselves outside of Myspace or Facebook. This was the birth of blogging as we know it.

As a content management system, WordPress is the leading website and blog platform. WordPress has two different platforms that work in similar ways. WordPress.org is free to use, however, you must have a host to house your WordPress website and blog content or files. The host would be a sort of cloud storage that houses and powers your site. Some of these include HostGator, GoDaddy, and 1and1. Each one provides their own type of hosting, along with an easy option to purchase a domain name for your website.

WordPress.com is also a free website content management system, but the difference is that with WordPress.com you are hosted under WordPress, with a site web address similar to wordpress.websitename.com or websitename.wordpress.com. At WordPress.org you have complete control, and only your imagination will limit you from designing the best website for your needs. Under WordPress.com you are limited to the available designs, themes, and plugins that are provided through their service. With WordPress.org you must have your own domain name and that would look similar to this: domainname.com.

Whichever WordPress platform you choose determines the customizable features and availability of using your creativity. If you want full control of the design, layout and customizable themes, then using WordPress.org is your best choice.

How to make it work for you.

To start a WordPress site, you will first need to have a domain name. These can be bought from any domain name server. Several companies have excellent reviews when it comes to purchasing and managing the registration information for the owner of that domain name. Domain names range in price from $1.00 for the first year all the way up to thousands of dollars, depending on what type of name you are purchasing and whether or not that name has a good Google page ranking. Google page ranking is a system by which websites are rated. Your Google page rank used to be the deciding factor on where your website was listed on Google search. With recent changes to the algorithms this has changed the importance of Google page ranking for websites, however, it is still a very important factor.

Each domain name provider has special services that they offer you when purchasing your domain name. These extra services sound good, however, they are not always necessary. It is often just a way to upsell you when you are buying your domain name. It doesn't matter where you buy your domain name from, whether it's the hosting company that is hosting your website, or another domain name purchasing company since they all provide the same services. However, you do need to pay attention to the price of the domain name after the first year of service. They can increase drastically depending on the special that was running when you purchased the domain name.

Each domain name is run on a yearly or multiyear purchase plan. You can purchase your domain name by the year or in multiyear increments depending on the amount they offer at check out and the company that you purchase from. The trick with a domain name is to remember when you registered it the first time and exactly 30 days before the due date, a year later, renew that name. As long as you are renewing your domain name before it expires, and the domain name hosting company is still in business, then you should have ownership of that domain name for the life of the purchase.

When you sign up for your domain name you will have to know what name you are wishing to use. Most people have been thinking about this for a long time, but if you haven't that is okay. Just know, that when you are exactly sure of what you want to name your website, that is when you should purchase your domain name.

Changing your website domain name after you have built your website will cause complications. It will end up being more work in the long run. It is best to have a domain name that you will want to have for the life of your business. Do not go for the generic domain name, but choose one that is brandable and unique. You should also limit it to six characters, as this makes it memorable. It should be easy to say and easy to remember. Once you have decided on your business or website name, your next step is to purchase that domain. Make sure you stick with the standard domain links such as .com, as well as, .net, and .org and avoid less common ones such as .name, .pizza, and any other suffix that they have come up with in the recent years. .com is the original and it is also the most trusted by people all over the world. The only exception to this rule is if you are international, in which case .co is okay. Otherwise, .com is the easiest for people to remember and most scam type companies us the unusual suffixes.

Domains are easy to come by and many people purchase domain names every day. Often times people buy several domain names that they may want to use in the future. They do this so that others don't take that name before them. By being selective with your name and checking the nameservers database, you can make sure that your name is available. After you have chosen your domain name and verified that it is available, you need to enter your details such as name, address, and billing information. This not only helps the company know who is opening the account and buying the domain but it also registers you as the owner in the icann registry service. This is the national domain name registrars site.

Picking a company to purchase your domain name from is the easiest part of the whole process. Next, you have to determine who you're going to use to host your website. Sometimes using the same company you bought your domain from to host your WordPress site is the best option. Sometimes a different company provides a better service. You do not have to use the same company, just make sure your host is a reputable company.

How do you pick a domain name?

Picking a domain name is not always the easiest thing to do. Often times you can just use your business name, however, if you do not have a business name or if you are just starting out, picking the domain is going to be hard. So, what do you do to pick a domain name?

- What are your passions or hobbies? When you are starting a new business or blog, going with something that is a passion of yours or a long time hobby is the best option for picking a domain name and content subject matter. There are several genres of blogging that can encompass everything, including cooking, travel, fashion, family, pets, cars, and even knitting. Whatever passion or hobby you have, think of how you can incorporate that into a website. Pick a name that goes along with this passion or hobby.

- Life experiences make for great content. There is always a lesson to learn in someone else's life experiences. Women who have survived horrible experiences, or men who have changed their gender, or even families dealing with disabilities all have something they can share with the world. As the old saying goes "one man's treasure is another man's junk". This holds true for life experiences as well. Your difficult life could be the saving grace to someone else dealing with something similar, especially if they are struggling and don't see any way out. Often times reading a book or article about a similar situation can mean the difference in giving up or staying strong.

- Personal blogs are all the rage with the younger generation. People are finding that they can blog about everything from food trucks to the latest gossip at school. Sometimes people will start blogging just so they can be heard. This often times turns into mom blogs or blogs all about living their life. A personal blog is another way to simply hear yourself talk, except you're talking to all your readers. A personal blog will include your daily thoughts, musings, and even your daily activities. It can be similar to your Instagram feed only with longer content.

Each one of these can give you an idea of how to find your domain name whether it is about you, yourname.com, or about a hobby, knittingwithyourname.com, or even a life experience, howtosurviveabuse.com. These are all connected to a purpose and a meaning. Domain names become the homes of our thoughts and without a good domain name, you are making it hard for others to know what to expect when they visit your site.

Make sure your domain name is descriptive and tells the potential readers what they can expect when they click on your link. For instance, if you are blogging only about the cars in Europe, then make the domain name express that, such as europeancars.com. Don't be too hung up on being specific with the subject matter in your domain name, as this could be limiting for how your site will evolve. For instance, a knitting site doesn't have to be knitting.com, it can be a popular technique for knitting or something that is relatable, such as yarnover.com or droppedstitch.com. Whatever you do, make sure your domain name makes sense to the content that is being written. Don't name your site strudel.com and write about chimpanzees.

Picking a hosting company

While you are looking for a hosting company, remember that there are many different features and styles of hosting. The hosting company that you pick is very important. Several hosting companies offer services that they do not deliver on. You want to make sure you are getting what you are paying for. If you purchase from a company with 99.99% up time, then you can expect to have little to no down time with your website. This is very important. Down time means that no one can see your website. If no one can see it, you are not reaching your target market. This hinders your bottom line and your Google page rank. Picking the right hosting company can be as simple or as hard as you make it. You definitely want something that will expand with your website, however, you do not want something that will cost you too much when you are just starting out. There are several hosting companies on the market that rank pretty highly among website builders and bloggers.

Here are just a few to pick from:

1. Bluehost has a load time of 419ms, an uptime of 99.99%, and costs $2.75 per month. Their live support has an average response time of 5 minutes, and this is very important when dealing with technical issues on your website.

2. HostGator is a cloud-based hosting company and has a load time of 462ms, with 99.96% uptime. They cost only $2.99 per month and the live customer support chat system has an average response time of 3 minutes, making this one faster at customer support.

3. SiteGround is the best WordPress hosting site on the market. It has 722ms for load time and an uptime of 99.99%. The monthly cost is $3.95, and the live support is boasting an average response time of 2 minutes. The faster you get to live chat for technical support can mean the difference between a complete crash and salvaging your website.

4. A2 Hosting is the fastest for shared hosting since the load time is ranked 3rd in the market at 413ms, and it has a 99.90% uptime. The cost per month is $3.92, but the live chat support is slower, at an average response time of 8 minutes. This can be troubling when you are stressing about technical issues for your website.

5. iPage is the cheapest option, coming in at $1.99 per month, and you truly get what you pay for. The load time is ranked 18th in speed at 868ms, with a 99.98% uptime. So, although your site is never down, the time it takes to load will deter possible buyers. The live chat support system has an average response time of 12 minutes. That is immensely slow when in desperate need of support.

6. GoDaddy has some of the best small business hosting reviews and only costs $2.49 per month. It loads at a 495ms speed and has an uptime of 99.96%, making it almost impossible for your site to be unavailable. The live chat support system is not the best since it averages a response time of 14 minutes.

7. FastComet is the best hosting company for web designers. It starts at $2.95 per month and has a load time speed of 1,083ms

making this site a super fast loader. The average uptime is 99.98% so you can be sure your site will be always up. The live chat response time averages 8 minutes, so it is not the fastest but it is still within a decent time frame.

If you are new to WordPress and website management, then you are probably wondering why we mention load time and uptime. This is because load time and uptime make a difference on how your traffic is getting to you and whether or not they are staying. Load time determines whether or not you are going to have a lot of bounce from people visiting your site. Bounce means that they visited your site and immediately left. Due to the speed that your website loads, your revenue from your website could be greatly reduced. If your website has a lot of downtime, then your target market is not able to view your website, and this can also put a damper on your revenue.

Once you find who you want to host your site with, you need to point your DNS for your domain to the new host's DNS servers. The DNS is what directs your domain name to the hosting company. This is usually the trickiest part of setting up your website. Your domain is your alias for your IP to your website. An IP address can look like this, 67.45.675.234, however, who is going to readily remember this? No one. So, we assign names such as wordpress.com to that IP address, making it easier for those trying to find our website. The DNS is the server that keeps track of where that name will take you. When you type in wordpress.org it will take you to the DNS directed site and that site will be the WordPress site. The company you buy your domain name from should be managing this, and they will allow you to edit or update your DNS. There are some DNS management companies that specialize in doing DNS services, however. One such company is DNS made easy. The IP address that this DNS points to is the one that the computer housing your website has assigned to your website.

It can take up to 24 hours for the DNS to propagate. What this means is that in order for that IP address to be the targeted point at which the domain name points, it must process through the system and be propagated. Usually, you can see results in under 8 hours and sometimes if they are struggling with propagation at the DNS server, it can take up to 48 hours, but the normal propagation time is around 24 hours.

Once your DNS is propagated, then you can start to work on your website.

How do you set up your WordPress site?

Now that you have done the steps up to this point, you may want to log in to your backend. This can be found inside your account at the company that you bought your hosting through. Each hosting company is different. Some of the backends are very different from others, but for general purposes, we are just going to talk about what you can find there. On the backend, you can find your website management system. This has a link to go to your c-Panel, as well as a way to make updates and changes to your billing and the features you purchased. The c-Panel is the control panel with which you run your website.

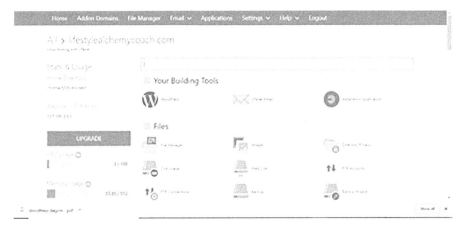

In your c-Panel, you will be able to download the WordPress software that will help you build your website. Most hosting sites provide a one-click install for WordPress, however, if they do not, below is listed two ways to install WordPress onto your dashboard.

The phpMyAdmin way of downloading WordPress in c-Panel

This will be located in the phpMyAdmin section. If you do not already have an existing database, although, most Linux systems do, you will need to just create one. First, you will choose a name relating to your WordPress, such as blog or WordPress. Most of the hosting providers will require something that starts with your username and an _ (underscore), such as tmasters_. You should enter your database name in the Create Database field. Next, choose the language and encoding that works best for you. The language should look something like this; utf8mb4_english_ci or something similar to your language preferences. Then, you need to assign a user if one isn't already on the Users tab. This has to be the user relating to the WordPress that you are setting up. If one isn't set up then click add user, and proceed to choose a username, entering it into the username field. Now you should choose your password and then re-type your password. Make sure you keep track of the username and password, as you will need them later. Leave all options as their defaults and click the go button. When that is done, click the user screen again and go to edit privileges. Start with the username you just created, click on database specific privileges, and select the add privileges to the following database option, and then click go. This will refresh your page at this time. Next, click all and select go again to set them up. Make a note of your host name listed after the server. This is located at the top of the page. Most the time it is localhost. This is just one way of downloading the WordPress platform to your site.

The MySQL way of downloading WordPress through c-Panel.

Locate the MySQL database wizard section of the c-Panel. You can find it under the icon for databases. Click on WordPress and start setting up your database. Next, you want to create your database by entering the database name. This should be what you identify the WordPress file by. Once you are done with that you need to set up your username and password. Then you click next at the bottom of the screen. This will install your WordPress and set up your database.

Make sure you check the All Privileges box for the database. Make sure you write down your user name and password and the web route for your database. This will be how you will access the c-panel to design your website.

Chapter 2

What You Need To Know
To Utilize It For Your Benefit

WordPress has many benefits for bloggers, website designers, as well as companies wishing to get online visibility. Some of those benefits can be explained by simply knowing that customization is an essential part of owning and running a successful and professional website.

WordPress can be both for business and personal use. If you are using it for business you can have a clean streamlined site that will hold all the important information you need for your customers to know what you do, how to contact you, your service agreement, testimonials, FAQS, locations, a price guide, recent activity for your business, coming sales, coming events, and so much more.

Not only can you provide details about your services and your company's history, but you can also provide details about the employees, such as the CEO, the CFO, Management, and the creative directors.

A business website has a wide range of benefits for the business and the customers looking to hire them. One of these benefits is the option to write a blog about your form of business. Every business has a focus, whether it is roofing or catering for events. There is a focus on a specific industry within every business. Even if you are a company with labor-based services, there is information that your clientele should know, such as how to take care of their new roof, or what to expect when getting a roof repair. If you are a catering company, you can blog about your events and how potential clients can properly prepare their event space for the caterers to have easy access to the things they need or even the types of catered parties that really are big hits for the client. There is always a market for information, so starting a blog is one of the added benefits to a WordPress website.

If you are not starting your WordPress site for a business, then you are probably starting it for a blog. Even if you are starting a personal blog, that doesn't mean that the same things a business would need will not apply. As with any well thought out blog, you will need a way to be contacted for readers and people who would like to collaborate with you, but you will also need information on the writer, or writers, of the blog, as well as information explaining why you started the blog. You could include a page about other people you support and even break your blog into sections. For instance, a food blog, which is not for a catering business, could have a section all about kitchen appliances that are amazing additions to the home, or recipes for specific genres of food culture. You could have a section on different places to experience different styles of food such as food trucks and street fairs, as well as tips and techniques for creating amazing dishes for family and friends. Whatever your focus is, there are several ways to make it work for you and your needs.

This book is going to be your go-to resource guide for building a WordPress website because inside this book is everything you need to know to make it work for you. Below is a short summary of what you will find in the rest of this book.

Summarizing this resource book is simple and can be broken down into 13 bullet points. Each bullet point represents one step you will take after reading this book so that you can build and set up your WordPress site and start blogging.

- Pick your domain name, research its availability and purchase it.

- Buy hosting from a reputable company and begin to set up your site.

- Transfer your DNS from the purchasing site's DNS to the hosting site's DNS.

- Download WordPress so that you can start building your website.

- Change or pick your theme out of thousands of professionally designed themes.

- Add in plugins that will support your website and protect it.

- Set up your website through the customization feature on WordPress.

- Design your website with a static page or blog page.

- Determine your genre for what you will use on your website, as well as the subject matter for your blog.

- Build pages for all your website content needs.

- Write posts that will entertain and educate your followers.

- Utilize some HTML for optimal blogging, so that your posts are optimized and elegantly written.

- Start blogging to build community, attract clientele, and reach those in similar situations.

Chapter 3

How To Change Your Theme
And Customize Your Site

WordPress has many different themes. When you first install WordPress on your hosting C-panel you will have a generic theme. This theme is named WordPress 2017.

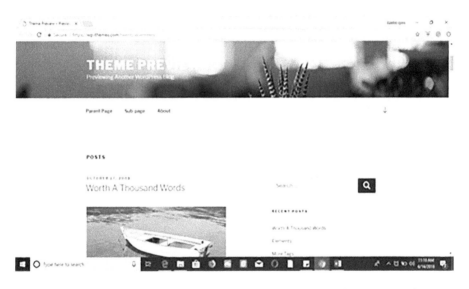

As you can see, it is pretty basic. The top piece is the Header image, and that is where the title of your website will go, as well as your menu. Underneath the header will be your posts or content section. Each WordPress theme is set up differently. Some have a focal point with three sections. These divisions are called side bars. You can have one or two side bars. Each side bar allows for you to include information such as widgets and plugins. Widgets are things such as a search bar, recent posts, authors profile, newsletter sign ups, site map, and social media links and more. Your content section this is where you would have your posts. Each post can be specifically designed with the title of the post, and the date it was published, along with images you may want to include.

At the bottom of the theme is your footer space. This space can contain widgets designed to display your contact information, your business address, and maybe a calendar of events or similar posts.

In your c-panel there is a side bar that shows your customization options as well as links for adding pages, posts, plugins, tools, and users. This is where you will find the appearance link for changing your theme. When you click on appearance, you get options for themes, customization, widgets, menus, headers, backgrounds, emails, edit CSS, and editor. Each one of these serves a purpose that is needed for designing a professional website.

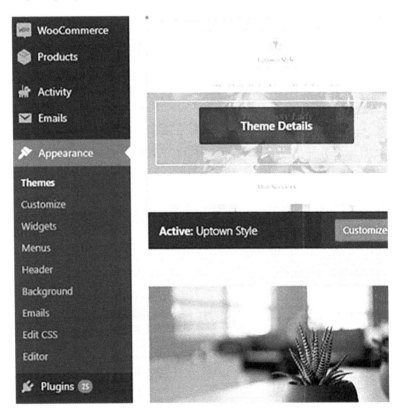

When you click on theme you get the option to add a new theme or pick from one of the themes that is already installed on your WordPress c-Panel. Since you do not want to look like everyone else's site on WordPress, you should find a theme that you like and that is unique for you.

To pick a new theme click on add new. This will take you to a screen with several options for picking a new theme. Each theme will have a preview option, so you can see it as if it was live on your site. There are over 1500 themes available for you, for free, through the theme link on your WordPress dashboard. If you want something unique and custom you can locate themes for WordPress at themeforest.com, and several other theme designer sites. All of these themes cost anywhere from $59.00 to $250.00 depending on who designed it. Although you can buy themes that are professionally designed, many of the free themes on WordPress are just as professional looking and just as well made. While in the theme section of your dashboard, use key words in the search bar to find exactly what you are looking for. For instance, if you are a photographer, you can search for photo, photography, gallery, or something similar to that. This will bring up all the themes linked to these keywords. Each theme is labeled with keywords that fit this specific design and purpose. So, finding a theme for your needs should be fairly easy.

To pick a specific theme, you can either search for it in the search bar or you can go to WordPress.org/themes. When you get there, find the theme that you like, then download the zip file. Once you download the zip file there is an option in your themes section that allows you to upload the theme into your WordPress c-Panel.

Once you have chosen your theme it will show up in your available downloaded themes. Do not worry about losing content, images, posts, or pages when you change your theme. You will be able to change your theme as much as you like without losing any details, content, pages, or posts.

22

Your next step is to click on the theme that you want to install into your WordPress site. Once you do this it will be available for customization and activation.

Next you want to click customize and start designing your WordPress website to your own specifications and design. By this time, you should have already designed a header or logo to use at the top of your Website. This helps those who come to your website to know who you are and what you are about. Choosing where to start is the first step to building your website. On the side bar there are 12 different options to begin with. Each one helps you customize that specific feature of your website. Listed below are the 12 different features you can customize in this area.

- Typography

- Site Identity

- Layout

- Colors

- Fonts

- Header Media

- Background Image

- Menus

- Widgets

- Homepage Settings

- Additional CSS

- Related Posts

Feature Options In Customization

Each feature has its own set of options to choose from. Most of them have several options. The typography section has an option to change the typography for each different part of the website. Typography is the font that you use for your content. You are able to choose a font from a pre-designated list of fonts, however, if you install a Google fonts plugin or the plugin "useanyfont", then you are giving yourself the option to use scripts not already available in the WordPress themes package. We will discuss plugins later in this book.

Colors

The colors section gives you the option to change the color scheme of your website, and this includes your content, headers, and background.

If you are unsure of the HEX codes for your color scheme, it would be a good idea to locate them. However, if you are not certain of what colors you would like to use, then the best thing to do is try out a few and see how you like them. It is a good idea to stick with colors that are on your logo, that way everything blends together smoothly.

Widgets

In the widgets section, you are able to install widgets to your website. For every theme, there will be pre-designated areas where widgets will go. This is based on the theme and type of widget. Each theme should have at least one footer section. In the footer section, you can apply whatever widgets you will need on your site. We will talk about widgets later in this book.

Site Identity

Site identity is where you will be able to insert your logo, your site title, and your tagline. A tag line is the motto of your company. For instance, if you are a lifestyle blogger you could use something like "healthy lifestyles for active moms", or something similar. You will also be placing your footer copywrite text in this section. The footer copywrite section is where you want to place the date you are establishing this business, or website, for instance, 2018, the copywrite symbol showing that it is a protected site, and the owner's name or business name. The next step in this section would be to design a site icon. This is the little icon that shows up in the tab that is above your domain name address bar.

Layout

Under the feature layout, you can find an option to make your page fixed or fluid. This is something that is up to you on how you make it. I generally use fluid for my websites.

Fonts

Under fonts, you will find a more specific list of fonts for more specific locations. This section pertains to your site title, navigation, headings, primary, and secondary fonts. Your primary fonts consist of the scripts used for paragraphs, lists, links, quotes, and tables. The secondary fonts consist of the typefaces for bylines, comment counts, reply links, post footers, and quote footers.

Header Media

Under header media, you are able to add a video if your theme allows videos in the header. If not, then this section allows you to add an image to the header. This is where you can insert an image to display what your business is all about. If you are a blogger you would use this for images that relate to the type of blog you are writing, for instance, a food blog would use delicious looking food images. If you are a business, you may want to display your business location or product line here.

Background

The background feature lets you place an image for your background. This is not necessary for most websites. Backgrounds are a way of displaying fun images for your readers, however, background images can be very distracting if not done tastefully. Most websites are going with a clean design and adding a background would detract from this.

Menus

The menus feature gives you the option to set up your menu, which helps readers to navigate your site. Each theme is different with their menu options. Some of them offer a top menu, and some offer two menus, one above the header and one below. Whether you have one menu or two, is not that important. The most important thing is to make sure the internal page links that you need for your readers to click on are in the menu. You should include several different links in this section.

- Home

- Contact us

- Services

- Blog

- About me

- Privacy page

- FAQ

- Specific pages for the type of service you offer; i.e., catering for a cook, weekend sitting for a babysitter, roofs for a construction or remodel company.

Making sure the readers have a direct link to your information, services, and contact details is the most important aspect of the website.

Home Page Settings

Homepage settings is another feature that you can customize here. Your homepage display has two options, one being your latest blog posts, and the other a static page with the specific information you need your readers to know. The next section to the homepage settings is to designate which page is going to be your homepage, and this can be your blog or your home. Then, you can designate what page should be your posts page, and there are several options here, based on what pages you have set up.

Additional CSS

Next, we have the additional CSS feature. This allows you to customize even further by setting specific CSS instructions for your website. CSS is a language that is used to tell the website what to display and how to display it. On this tab, you can click on the link to learn more about CSS and figure out ways to further customize your website outside of the normal drag and drop parameters.

Chapter 4

WordPress Plugins
That You Should Get To Know

WordPress has a ton of plugins. Plugins are tools that can be used to enhance or allow your website to work with other business tools. For instance, a MailChimp plugin will work towards integrating your newsletter sign up form with your website. Each plugin serves a function; however, you have to be careful with the plugins you place into your c-Panel. There are often several plugins for the same exact service. So, check the reviews before using one and make sure the plugin you choose does exactly what you need it to do. You also want to make sure it is a plugin that is updated regularly.

In this chapter, there are detailed descriptions and usage options of some of the most downloaded plugins that are necessary for a smoothly running business website.

1. Add to any share buttons

2. Akismet Anti-spam

3. All in one WP Security

4. Antispam Bee

5. Beaver Builder Booster

6. Beaver Builder Plugin

7. Broken Link Checker

8. BuddyPress

9. Contact Form 7

10. Contact Widgets

11. Disqus for WordPress

12. Easy Google Fonts

13. Elementor

14. Genesis Simple Edits

15. Genesis Simple Share

16. GoDaddy Email Marketing

17. Google Analytics for WordPress

18. Google XML Sitemaps

19. IceGram

20. Instagram Feed

21. Jetpack

22. Limit Login Attempts

23. Mailchimp for WordPress

24. Ninja Forms

25. Pretty Links

26. PB SEO Friendly Images

27. Subscribe Button

28. TinyMCE Advanced

29. Updraft Plus- Backup/Restore

30. Woocommerce

31. WP Popular Post

32. WP Related Posts Thumbnail

33. WP Broken Link Status Checker

34. WP Fastest Cache

35. WP Retina 2x

36. WP Optimize

37. Yoast SEO

These are just a few of the ones that I have used for my WordPress website over the past few years.

Now I will go over exactly what a few of these are used for and why they are important to your WordPress website.

PB SEO

PB SEO friendly images are one of the plugins listed in the suggested list of useful plugins which are important for a professional website.

This plugin helps you to optimize your images with an ALT and Title attribute in your posts. These are important for your website-ranking. It helps for your site to be more easily located with all search engines.

Smush

Smush is an image compression and optimization plugin that is used in WordPress sites. It helps to resize, optimize, and compress all your images for your WordPress site. Hosts only give you so much storage, and images tend to take up quiet a lot of storage. This plugin will help minimize the space that images are using. You are able to reduce the image size without losing the quality of your image. Images that are large can slow down your site and you wouldn't even know it. Instead, download Smush and you will not have to worry about this again. It will instantly "smush" your images down to a size that is designated from when you installed and set it up.

Broken Link Checker

Broken Link Checker is a wonderful plugin that checks your blog automatically without any extra work from you, to see if there are any broken links in your content. It monitors links in your posts, pages, comments, the blogroll, and custom fields. It detects links that are missing images, redirects, and links that don't work. It will notify you through your dashboard as well as email. Not only does it check for broken links, but it also prevents search engines from following those links, and you can edit the links from the plugin, and filter your links by URL.

Yoast SEO

Yoast SEO is an SEO optimization plugin. Yoast adds specific functions to your website that helps you improve your search engine ranking and allows for organic searches to find your site. This is the most comprehensive SEO plugin, and it is great for blogs as well as professionals managing other's SEO of their websites. It gives you the control of titles, meta descriptions, target keywords, and tracking how often you use them. It helps you maintain your sitemap and many other things.

Akismet Antispam

Akismet Antispam is pre-installed on your WordPress site as soon as you download WordPress. However, it does have to be activated to be used. It is a comment spam filtering system. What this means is it catches pingback spam as well as blog comments that use the algorithm they designed. This algorithm learns when mistakes are made and acts to correct them. It also learns from the interaction with other websites that have downloaded it and instills those changes into its platform. Using akismet helps free up your time by blocking spam comments without interfering with your legitimate comments. So far Akismet has caught more than 83 billion spam comments.

WP Contact Widget

WP Contact Widget is a great way to have contact with your readers and customers, or potential customers. This is a simple tool that will be easy to install on your site. It is a drag and drop feature, and you can create a custom form that will help your potential customers and readers to be in contact with you if they need to.

MailChimp WP

MailChimp WP is a great way to integrate your Mailchimp newsletter form into your site. Not only does it provide you with a great way to have subscribers or newsletter signup's, but it also helps you to have customized forms so that each subscriber can sign up for a specific newsletter. They can also sign up for one newsletter or several by simply filling out a form on your website.

Elementor

Elementor is a page builder plugin for your WordPress blog. It allows you to have seamless results on the front end of your site. You are able to design at record speed without having to drag and drop and then wait to see how it looks. It instantly shows your changes, providing you with the freedom to customize without coding. You can change the layout of the front end page or even add new features.

Contact Form 7

Contact Form 7 is a great way of adding a seamless format for your customers to contact you. With Contact Form 7 you can add this feature to any portion of your website. For instance, say you want a contact form on your about me page. Then add in the code for the previously designed Contact Form 7 and place it on the page you want, making sure it is in text mode when placing the form. The text is where you can add in <h1> tags and they will show properly in your post.

Google Analytics

Google Analytics is the go to analytics tracking site. Analytics are tracked based on the number of visitors to your site, the bounce rate, and the unique visitors that have visited your site. They also keep track of the geographical location for the visitors that come to your site. But that's not all, you also get details of what they searched for to find your site and how long they stayed on your pages.

Chapter 5

Designing Your Website With WordPress

Now that you have your theme designed, it is time to start laying out your website. To start with, pick the pages you would like to have on your website. This can be any number of pages, however, you will definitely need an about me page, a contact me page, services (if you offer any), and a FAQs and privacy policy page.

You can start by clicking on pages on the sidebar and add a new page. Once you have figured out which page you want to add, label that page with the title of what it represents or what its purpose is. This is where things start to get more technical. You will open on a page that has a title bar at the top with a tools section that is similar to the tool bar in Microsoft word. Under the tools you will find the space for the content.

Below the content space, you will find that there are several different things that you can use to customize your pages, such as Yoast SEO if you downloaded it. To the right-hand side, you will have the section that says publish with a date and time. It also provides you with an option to schedule this page to be published at a later date when you are not available to publish it. If you want your new page to be linked to it in the menus bar, then click appearance and then select menu in the menu section. After that, click whatever page it is that you want to add to the menu and click add to the menu. One option that is available for posts and pages is to have a featured image. This is an image that, when the content is displayed in bit size pieces of the content, will be featured at the top of the post.

Follow these steps to continue to add pages to your menu and to add in pages on your blog. Next, you will want to start adding posts. Posts are what we call blogs and will contain the current content for your site. They are the meat and potatoes of the website. Developing categories will help you keep your posts organized. For instance, you can categorize every blog post as "blog" and then tag them with the subject matter or keyword that you are targeting. When you write your posts, there will be a section where you can add them to a category, as well as insert tags into the post, so that it will be organized accordingly. To create categories, go to posts and then click on categories. Another way to create categories is to create a blog post by clicking on the post and then clicking on add new.

Once you click on add new you can give it a title and even a custom sub-URL for the blog post and then write the content that you wish to publish. Blog posts usually have a URL similar to domainname.com/blog-post/, and this can be customized when you are in the post, so take the time to make your URL look good. When writing the post, you will need to include keywords. Keywords are the words that attract the readers to your post. When someone types into Google the keyword toothpaste, their search results come up with posts that contain, or are tagged with, the keyword "toothpaste". If your company is about toothpaste, you want to be on that list. You want to be on the first page so that you will get the most traffic to your site. The more traffic, the higher the analytics, and once you have a good bit of traffic, you can also start to build a profit from your blog.

The page title will explain to search engines and those who search Google, what your article or blog post is about. Without a good page title, you will not get traffic. Page titles are also the way the search engines rank your website. If you do not organically include your keywords, you will struggle in getting noticed. Keywords are words that are searched often. You want to be using ones that relate to your field and are widely used in searches. You also want to only use ones that you are using in your content. For instance, you don't use the keyword essential oils, and then have a whole article about prescription drugs. That would be false and misleading.

Often times people will write a negative review on something but place a positive twist on the title and then include the keyword of whatever they are reviewing into the content and the title. This can be misleading for so many people and is often termed as click-baiting. For instance, say a blog is titled "Essential Oils: The Miracle Cure". Then, throughout the content, the article may mention essential oils, but it discredits them and talks in a negative tone about them. This is misleading since the reader was probably looking for a real article on how they are the miracle cure. Now, they are reading an article that is contrary to what the reader was actually searching to find.

Remember that however, you word your title will determine if people actually read your article. Sometimes you may get comments that are not to nice. You can opt out of comments for your posts and pages by going into the page you want, and turn off the comments option by clicking screen options in the top right-hand corner. Once you click this, you will see a discussion box inside that one. You will find a hot button to allowing comments, and you can simply unclick allow comments and it will no longer accept comments on that page.

If you want to disable comments on your page by default, then simply go to settings and then discussion. Under the default article settings, there will be a section that says allow people to post comments on new articles. Simply unclick that box, and then save the change.

Static Page

Earlier we discussed static pages. But what exactly is a static page? A static page is simply a page that stays the same, unlike blog pages, which are always current and updated with the new information you are posting. It has a main central theme with information or one specific bit of content that is design ed to welcome the new readers to your page. It is a page that never changes. To create a static page, you will need to go to settings and then reading. Choose the static page option and choose the page that you have previously set up that you would like to use as the static page. This is usually your home page. The current blog will be the page that is the home page of your blog if you choose to have a static page instead of a blog homepage.

Chapter 6

Writing A Blog With WordPress

Many times, people have asked how to write a blog. The simple answer is you just sit down and write, sort of like a journal that you are sharing with the world. But, it isn't really that simple. First, you have to have a web platform on which to write a blog. That is where WordPress comes in. Inside your WordPress you have a section called posts. This section is where you can write your blog posts. If your website is specifically a blog, then in your customization you can make your home page your recent posts. However, if your website is for a business, you may want to have your blog as a secondary page. How you design your website layout is up to you.

What exactly is a blog?

A blog is a form of a website that is focusing on mainly written content, however, it can also contain images you incorporate into your posts. Often times, blogs are written from a personal perspective and contain content that the writer feels are important to tell others. There are blogs about celebrities, news, politics, food, medicine, hair care, lifestyles, children, pets, and so much more.

When you are writing articles for the main purpose of entertaining or educating others, it is a blog. Anyone can start a successful blog. All it takes is the determination to educate or entertain others through words, and a few key ingredients which we are discussing int this resource book.

Since bloggers often write from their own perspective, blogs tend to be personal. Some would call them a personal live journal. However, not all blogs are journal related, nor are they all opinion pieces. The blogs that are written to promote a certain lifestyle or which discuss specific events in history tend to be based in evidential, researched, and cited proof. So, you don't have to be writing about something from a perspective of self. It can be about a factual situation and be more scientifically based.

Bloggers generally write in informal ways. They tend to write conversational style posts. Most of them are not even good writers. The misconceptions about blog writing are that you have to be formal, and you have to have an extensive knowledge of English grammar. But this is far from the truth. The readers of blogs are just like the writers. They are everyday people who feel that they have the knowledge they wish to share with the world. Whether it is for educational purposes, opinions, celebrity gossip, recipes for specific cultures, diet plans, or just as a way to express their story, it is all acceptable in the blogging world.

There are many forms of blogs and with WordPress, you are able to write any type of blog you choose, whether it's a travel blog with mostly images or a recipe blog, you have the freedom to be creative. Blogs have become the best way to connect with your customers for businesses and a great way to express yourself when you have so much that you want to say. It is the first step that many authors take before writing a book. There are blogs that range in subject matter from auto mechanics to custom cloth diapers. If you can imagine it, you can bet there is a blog about it.

Blogging has helped those who can not be published find their 15 minutes in the spot light by writing their thoughts online. The best thing about blogs is that you do not have to be an expert at all. Many people can share your views, even if you have opinions are that are only based on partial facts, so finding your crowd will not be hard. Those who follow a mom blog do not want to hear about all the positives of being a mom. They want to her about the ups and downs, the pain, the rewards, and your own reality. They want to be able to read the blog and say you are not alone. They want the mistakes and the accomplishments. They want to feel connected to the bigger picture. To be a successful blogger you have to be passionate about your subject.

In most blogs, there is a comments section that allows the readers to communicate with the writer. By interacting with your readers, you are involving them in the exchange of content and it helps them become loyal followers, and to build a community. This helps grow your readership and your revenue from your WordPress site in the long run.

Writing your blog with WordPress

Writing your blog with WordPress makes it easy to write. Yes, there are many sites out there that provide a free blogging platform. The difference between WordPress and those other sites is that with WordPress, you own all your material. What this means is that the site can not shut you down and keep your content. It is yours to keep. You can back your site up every day if you like and it will send you a file to upload in the event that your site crashes. This is an important step to writing with WordPress. Always have a backup, just in case the site crashes. Another important step to developing a blog with WordPress is to burn your feed with feedburner. Feedburner is an RSS feed system that allows subscribers to read your content on a type of newsfeed page. They will get all the feeds for the blogs they follow, on a newsfeed page similar to Facebook's newsfeed page.

This will allow your followers to either sign up for a newsletter or to simply add you to their newsfeed. It makes it easier for them to have access to your content, allowing you to reach more people with your knowledge and message. Another advantage to writing your blog with WordPress is that you can set up Google analytics as well as setting up your SEO protocols so that you are receiving more visitors.

Not many blog platforms provide an easy SEO solution. WordPress has an easy SEO platform, once you understand what SEO is and how to use it.

How to write a blog post

Once you have opened a new post in your WordPress dashboard you will want to focus on writing a blog. Your first step is to make sure you are using the visual mode. This is a tab located in the tools section, similar to Microsoft word tools. It is to the right-hand side and there is one that says visual and one that says text. You want to choose visual because it is the proper formatting that you will need for headings, bold, italics, centering, so what you see is what you will post. Once you have verified that it is in the visual mode you will need to click on the tab that is called kitchen sink. This button is located second to last on the tools bar. It is three past the link symbol. This will allow for more formatting options to open. Some of these include underlining, change font color, add a heading and so on. Now that you have all your tools ready it is time to write your post.

Start with your title. This will give you a basic idea of what you are trying to say in this post. Don't worry too much about this, though, since your title isn't set in stone until you publish it. If you find yourself writing and the content heads in a new direction, just edit your title before you publish. Do make sure your titles are catchy and a bit of fun. They should also be on topic and have keywords.

Your keywords should also be used within the first sentence of your article. This ensures that the Google bot is going to find this article and place it in any searches for that keyword. Now, once your blog post is written, go back and edit your permalink. The permalink is the link that takes you directly to that blog post. Use your keywords. Try to make it as close to a search term as you can. Instead of using something like /oils-brand-best/, use /best-oil-brands/. You want to use words that would be searched for in the same specific order.

One of the final steps is to create links to your post, as well as adding pictures. To add your media to the post, you should find the spot where you want to place the media and click so that your cursor is in that spot. Then click on the add media button. Next, locate your media from your computer or your pre-existing files in your WordPress storage. If you are not the owner of the media, make sure you have permission to use the images. This can be done in several ways. One way is to get written permission from the owner. Another way is to get your images from a content mill site like pixabay.com or shutterstock.com. Remember that you cannot just take an image off the internet unless it says Creative Commons or CCO. You can find several websites that send you copyright free images every month through email.

Next, you should create links to your posts that are internal. Internal means that you are linking back to your own content. By highlighting the word, you want to link and clicking the little symbol that looks like a chain link, you are able to add internal or external links.

Once you have added all the media and links to your post that you want to, now you need to select the category that it should be linked under. This is also when you add your tags. On the right side of the screen, you have an option to select the categories that you wish to organize this post under. It also has a place for you to use tags for locating this post inside those categories. Choose the ones you want for organizational purposes.

Now you are ready for the post to be published. However, maybe you don't want it published right away. If you are scheduling the post, choose the day and time you wish it to go live on your website. If you are ready to publish it, then click publish and if you are not ready to schedule or publish it, click draft. In this same box, you can make this post private, as well as password, protect it.

Now you may ask why you would make it private or password protected. Well, for many reasons. Private posts can be posts that you wrote but are not ready to share with the world. Maybe you just wanted to get the post written but not are unsure of sharing it with anyone else just yet, and this would mean that you want to make it private. If you have a subscription page for people to subscribe to certain content and charge some money for that content, then that is another reason why you would make it password protected. Anyone with the password could then access it but not people who just casually view your site. Password protection is a great way to create an e-course through your website or to have a paid resources page.

The difference between visual and text mode on the post editor.

In visual editor, you are seeing the text as it will appear. In text mode, you are seeing the text with the codes in it. There are many codes that can be used in text mode.

Listed below are several of the popular text codes that can and should be used in WordPress.

- **B** -<strong></strong>bold

- *I* -<italics></italics>italics

- b-quote -<blockquote></blockquote>block quote

- del -<del></del>strike through or deleted

- link -<a href=http://example.com></a>link

- ins -<ins></ins> <u>underlined text</u>

- ul- -<ul></ul>bulleted list

- ol -<ol></ol>numbered list

- li -<li></li> list item

- code -<code></code>preformatted styling of text

- More -<!—more→breaks a post into "teaser" and content sections. This produces a more link for those posts where you have a short paragraph with more button.

- Page -<!—nextpage→same as the more tag but can be used an unlimited number of times in the post. This breaks up the post.

- Lookup -opens a JavaScript search box.

- Close tags -closes any open HTML that is left open.

Now you know how to write your first post. You have learned all about WordPress and how you, too, can use it to help you build a website or blog. Now it is time to start putting this resource book to action and start sharing your knowledge and opinions with the world.

Why do people blog on WordPress?

Many people blog so they can express their opinions to the world. However, there are other reasons to blog. Several of these reasons are listed below.

1. To make extra money from home. Not many people realize that blogging can be a great way to bring in extra money. If you make it a full-time job and get many collaborators, sponsors, or

associate links, you can essentially turn blogging into a money-making machine. Since blogging does not require many hours of commitment a day, it can be a great way to work from home, making money and still spending time with family and friends.

2. Sharing your story is another reason to blog. Many people have lived through some tough times. Some of them have been survivors of natural disasters and war crimes. Telling your story could help someone else who is dealing with a similar situation. Women who are infertile will blog to find community and parents blog to share their worries and concerns in child rearing, as well as their joys.

3. Business recognition is another reason to blog. When you have a business, it is a great option to start a WordPress site that is geared around your business and the knowledge that others would need to know that pertain to your business.

4. Finding a like minded community is something that draws many bloggers into blogging. Because blogging is highly interactive, it is a great way to meet people that are interested in the same things that you are interested in. Community can come in all forms and blogging is a great way to find one.

Conclusion

Thank you, for making it through to the end of *WordPress: Basic Fundamental Guide For Beginners*. Let's hope it was informative and able to provide you with all of the tools you need to achieve your goals, whatever they may be.

The next step is to figure out what you are most passionate about. Once you have figured out what you are passionate about, find a domain name or business name that fits that genre. Check online and make sure that the domain name is available and, if so, purchase it so that you can start to build your very own WordPress blog. WordPress is an advanced platform for business websites and blogging. With this resource book, you should be well on your way to building an amazing website that can help you achieve all your website dreams. From the knowledge that you will gain from this resource book, you should have a great basis to start you on the right path. Your knowledge of HTML should be expanded upon after reading this resource guide and there should be no question as to where to get started with building your website using WordPress

Finally, if you found this book useful in any way, a review on Amazon is always appreciated!

www.ingramcontent.com/pod-product-compliance
Lightning Source LLC
Chambersburg PA
CBHW070901070326

40690CB00009B/1942